The Lenten Moon
Copyright © 2018 by Helen Morrissey Rizzuto
ISBN 978-0-692-12432-1

All rights reserved. No portion of this book may be reproduced, stored in an electronic retrieval system, or transmitted in any form or by any means — electronic, mechanical, photocopy, recording, or any other — except for brief quotations in printed reviews, without the prior written permission of the author.

THE LENTEN MOON

La Luna Cuaresmal
Una Oracion
by
Helen Morrissey Rizzuto

*...Und in den Nachten fallt die schwere Erde
aus allen Sternen in die Einsamkeit...*

*Und doch ist Einer, welcher dieses Fallen
unendlich sanft in seinen Handen halt.*

...And through the night the heavy earth falls too,
down from the stars, into the loneliness...

Yet there is one who holds us as we fall
Eternally in his hands' tenderness

from Herbst, Autumn
<u>Selected Poems</u>
Rainer Maria Rilke

Also by Helen Morrissey Rizzuto

POETRY

Evening Sky On a Japanese Screen

A Bird in Flight

in the dark curfew'd streets
Long Beach, Long Island in the aftermath...

NONFICTION

American By Choice, One Man's Journey
with Alfredo Fuentes, former Battalion Chief F.D.N.Y,
Survivor of the 9/11 attacks on the World Trade Center

with gratitude to the religious, both living and deceased,
who inspired this small collection, especially

>
> Rev. Patrick J. O'Connor
> Rev. James Earlis Quinn
> Rev. Joseph Wiseman
> Rev. Francis Pullo
> Rev. William D. Lyons
> Rev. Robert E. Kennedy, S.J.

the Jesuits who taught Apologetics at Marymount School
Sister Germaine Alida, SUSC

and
Saint Padre Pio

dedicated to

His Holiness Pope Francis
Papa Francesco

Elements

The Lenten Fair	page 10
mite box	page 11
Relic	page 13
Repository	page 14
Vigil Light	page 15
The Lenten Moon	page 16

Saints

Lives of the Saints	page 18
Beyond Luke's Account, "*The Pardon of the Sinful Woman*"	page 19
The Gift	page 21
The Office	page 24
by lamplight	page 25
The Revenant	page 26

The Women

Mary	page 28
near Ephesus, at Mary Magdalene's table	page 30
…and, Joseph	page 32

the Alpha and the Omega

Jesus and the Birds	page 34
when He spoke	page 35
the ALPHA and the OMEGA	page 36
Learning to Listen	page 37

ELEMENTS

The Lenten Fair

How strange it is
To fall in love each year
With the same melancholy stranger
Of a season

To pass the tattered tents of childhood
Their flaps still snapping in the wind
Where mystics and misers
Showgirls and saints
First swayed
        the mind
and mined gold

The dark
Is a cocoon this night
Dim with amber lanterns
        and stained-glass windows
Cast flames
Onto hardened ground

A shadow flickers
On the station wall, and
As you watch, you wonder
Why, in this boarded up shaft

Is the soul that so longs
To dance
At last, content

Where is the cupped flame
In whose hand

mite box

I

we learned the sacrifice
even before we took to the field
our awkward hands
trained in how to frame the *mudra*
our fingers quietly disciplined
into form

folding manila flaps
of cardboard strips
to form the walls of a house

led us to grasp
the architecture in our already able fingers

each week, we watched
as pennies, nickels, dimes
and quarter
first audible, later more subdued,
slipped through
the slot in the 'roof'
to the 'floor'

walls expanded, and when
they could hold no more,
these cardboard mansions
we had filled with allowances
made their way to *missions*

to cousins whose streets were not lit with lamps
or trimmed with penny roses or the music of
ragman or elevated train
pulling into the station at dusk

yes, all that year, if we put our ear to
the wall of recent memory
we could hear the scraping of wooden spoons
against the bellies of wooden bowls
far off

THE LENTEN MOON

capturing the last of the porridge
that had rained down there

II

years later, when
those mite boxes became articles
of derision, missiles aimed at the silly
notions of children
who believed they could change
the world
with food in its humblest form –
though the great Russian figure of letters
would be praised
for suggesting the same –

I would recall the wooden floors
the wheezing radiators, the glaring
hanging lamps of those old-fashioned
classrooms and cupboards
their paste and paper, their innocence
curled like carpenters' shavings

I would remember the nuns
and I would see again

how we all had loved
making *something*
out of *so very little:*

a difference
ourselves

[for Venerable Fulton J. Sheen]

Relic

the word, when I first heard it,
sounded archaic, like parchment
being scratched by a quill, and

try as I will to open my mind
even now, throw open the shutters
to let in the light and accept the reality
that all was *perhaps*
and not *as,* I fail

content instead, to curl up
inside this artifact-memory
from my desert youth —

the priests always visited
in the evening, and I could never tell
if they brought mystery with them
or if mystery followed them, the way
twilight follows day and
            lingers like incense
long after the last *Te Deum* has been sung

in the end
their fragile gifts
born in the past, housed now
in glass,
drew me in

sliver of bone
patch of faded muslin
splinter of wood on swatch of red

this last consumed me, and
I disappeared
into what I held in my hand:

jeering mob, insensate road
      weary, bloodied forlorn step

the tree we nailed Him to in the end

Repository

Holy Thursday
   Evening

the loneliest
word of the year
always appeared
when those
wooden clappers
cracked the air

the shock
hammering
those nails
into flesh
wood, memory
bone

tore open
the ark of emptiness
inside

an emptiness so vast

that the craving desert
the moonless sky
the lifeless sea
might as well
never have been filled

He was gone

Vigil Light
sanctuary lamp

those of us who sat at the bedside
of our dying mothers
night after night, hour stitched to passing hour –
a patchwork of orphans staving off time –

came to know
those sanctuary lamps
that burn through the dark
on church altars in every quarter

and at roadside shrines
along country roads

those spectral notes that drift down
every saxophone-haunted
rain-slicked city street

all the world's lamps

that tell the passer-through
he is not alone

are you

*There was a child went forth every day
and the first object he looked upon and received with wonder or
pity or love or dread, that object he became
and that object became part of him...*
                                        Walt Whitman

The Lenten Moon

a light is burning in the upstairs
of this painting, a painting that spans
the length of the wall

the first I would come to know in a long
list of unknowns

it hung in the stark morning stillness,
and at lunchtime over scattered pages and
small bologna sandwiches on Arnold's rolls

long after dusk
when all of us would finally
sit down for dinner, the painting remained

a boarder no one ever mentioned
a silent witness to all that transpired under that roof
but a presence, all the same

its deep blue garden of olive trees and shadows,
rocks and bramble, cloud crossing moon

blessed the night as the house slept

in a world of skirmish, illnesses and deaths,
the one constant
even as I lay awake each night upstairs
steeling myself for her final breath and
the funeral cortege winding its way
through another Calvary, another
    vale of tears

was the man praying
    always praying under the Lenten moon
in the silent blue garden, downstairs

SAINTS

Lives of the Saints

We make them beautiful
On the carousels of our minds
Each steed a porcelain replica
Galloping to the finish

Steam wheezing through its pipes
The calliope fires
And they're off

From the wild and weedy lots
Of their beginnings
Our work begins

Jairus's fragile daughter
Is only sleeping we say, her hair,
The magnificence of midnight, falls undone
Like Giselle's, after the peasant girl has gone mad,
And her olive skin still glistens
Even as life withdraws

Those two pensive travelers
On the road to Emmaus
One handsomer than the other
Their robes the perfection
Of holy cards or Hollywood
Are nothing like the Jewish men who
Sit beside us on the train

And Timothy sent off for circumcision
Never objects, never tells Paul *no*
He simply disappears behind a specialist's door
Far from the torn tent
Where the *mohel* waits, sharp blade
In calloused hand

Inside our solitary cells
we reconstruct them all

hammering
       into the deepest part of night

Beyond Luke's Account
"The Pardon of the Sinful Woman"
    Luke 7, 36:50

at Bethany
in the dim after-dinner din
amid the music and clatter of stoneware
and wood-smoke rising
it was easy for her to enter

she found him right away
and took no notice of those who knew her
to be out of place
she must have knelt, must have kissed
the sandaled feet that knew well
the ruts of roads, the rocks, the fallen
broken twigs of wind-formed trees

even before the tears, there must have been
this kiss, because he was so different
from those who had taken
her, had drawn on her breasts
until rough hands and blinding ecstasy had formed
the vise her moans stole through

lovers who, in the end, had abandoned her and
silenced her tongue
in the tomb her mouth had become

here, the young rabbi reclined
at ease in the moment, wanting
nothing

she wasn't tentative
in her touch, her knowing fingers
perused the instep, stroked the weary
ligaments and tendons
read the braille of bone, traveled the five tributaries
branching down into metatarsals, until
his feet became easy in her hands
that understood so well the fragile workings of a man

THE LENTEN MOON

she used the hands he had given her
and as she gathered up her hair
in the silken honeyed light
to dry his feet
he must have closed his eyes…

at the arc of the narrative, the moment's
brutal beauty
when she shattered the alabaster flask
and let loose her perfume

rubbing the ointment into his feet
flesh to flesh, tongue of flame
to fire
he must have surrendered

as he would again
on Golgotha

The Gift
[on the eve of canonization]

This story isn't one you've heard before
very few seem to recall now
that he was a man the Church kept hidden
in her folds, during those dark days after the war
to cloak him from Satan who
it was said might have carved
his initials
very different from the Lord's
into the man's hands

We've all seen pictures
of those hands
wrapped for mass in layers of gauze
and those brown woolen gloves
without the fingers
One sepia print taped for years
to the mirror of the Italian bakery
on the avenue is still there
but back in those days, no one
in the neighborhood
dared mention his name

and why would I care
child that I was
sitting up each night, bartering
with God to spare my young mother

promising never to close my eyes
or stop praying, *ever*,
if He would just keep her alive
and assure me the geography of the room,
the only country that concerned us,
would continue to accommodate the shadows:
the oxygen tanks in the corner
the mask, the brace, the bottles of pills by the bed
I'd hardly heard of Italy, much less
some obscure Italian priest
living in its hills

THE LENTEN MOON

but life has a way of redressing itself
of drawing together coordinates
of the unlikeliest origins
and long before Rome and his consecration
I would meet the man with bleeding hands

September crept into October
that year and November stood
like a sentinel on the porch
when the envelope finally arrived
with its trim white scalloped bodice
I always recalled later as blue
    my name
written in an elegant foreign hand

the nun who had risked her calling
had divulged only that there was a man
she knew who could help my mother
I must write
and wait for word

but the envelope newly arrived
was too ordinary to house hope
even now, I remember the taste
of despair as two holy cards
one in English, the other, Italian
and two printed strips of vellum*
slipped to the floor

I was searching for fire
or the neon-blue magic of ice
an apparition like a genie
isn't that how miracles would appear?
something extraordinary to assure me
my mother wouldn't die that year

but truth often waits in silence
and whispers things we might not wish to hear

the road my mother stumbled along
was strewn with mines, but held
eight autumns more

THE LENTEN MOON

So, as Rome prepares its banquet
and those he touched, and those he is said
to have visited, pack their bags for the flight
I'm drawn again to a lonely road
where a young girl once stood alone, and

it isn't prayer-cards or miracles or
even the prospect of his sainthood I envision
but a man who took time
for a child he didn't know
and walked beside her in the twilight
and held her hand

* *"Padre Pio will pray for your intentions"*

the Office

this evening, in the shadow of
the church steeple and
overhanging el
as the N train brakes to a squealing halt

and a famous rock star's mother
switches on the lamp in the apartment
to spend the night waiting out
her grandchild's entrance
onto this planetary stage

the spirits of other Friday evenings
convene as they always convened
in those waiting rooms
when I was a child... sometimes

I still see them on the street
milling outside the door

this is the place I came to know
my father best, the stern enforcer
of upstairs rules, down here
would thaw, and someone else
would take his place

in that surgical coat, behind a face that had
come to terms with the grave,
he greeted the dying and soon-to-be
born, greeted bishop and beggar,
sinner and saint alike, held them
and healed them

each evening, after the last dark window had been lit
the last goodnight uttered on the wind
he tucked them all away
prayerbeads and boarders, memories and intentions
and then made his way upstairs

by lamplight
for the woman who cured blindness at BC

brilliance
is a word we reserve for stars,
moon, those wind-tossed lanterns
that light the porches
of celestial gods

before her own was
snuffed out, her brain cordoned off,
quarantined from the rest of her
and declared dead

my friend
wore her brilliance modestly

it shone in
a turn
of phrase
a knowing nod
a laugh that shamed
the morning
birds and turned their music
to chatter

now, when we long for just
the utterance of one of those
Latin syllables, those verdant Greek phrases,
the voice as deep and quiet
and wise
as the river's at dusk

when we feel the tug of all those
long-gone autumns, the conversations
curling into evening like piety or smoke
we must close out the light
and listen...

    [for Margaret Landry]

The Revenant

He would arrive before midnight
Like the dark and like the wind on those
Nights when the moon sails behind
The bare branches of trees and you feel
The presence of old long absent friends

I loved the knocking against glass
When the wood of the door refused to give
I loved the steady tapping, the heavy brogue
The defiance and insistence at that late hour
To be let in, and how my father, inflexible as time,
Would order the lights dimmed

The battle, the continued mock refusal to relent on either side
And the way, in the end, we would have to yield and
How only then, at that late hour, the party would begin.
Once, he went back to the land he'd been forced
To leave and brought me back a china doll, an
Irish version of Red Riding Hood in emerald
And porcelain, and when it came time,

And without his knowing, I took his rebel name and tucked it
Safely between my own. After he'd gone for good -
Beyond the land of green hills and mists and glens – on
A summer day when all the trees were still
The music stopped. We didn't play a song
That entire year, as if we needed silence
To reinvent him,
            to hear his steady rapping at the door.

[for Rev. Patrick J. O'Connor]

THE WOMEN

*...in the sixth month, the angel Gabriel was sent
from God to a town of Galilee called Nazareth...*
Luke I 26-28

Mary

in the blinding white sunlight of morning
he came, not with the beating of wings
or on a rush of wind that
ruffled the water and announced him,
there was no warning...

                      he appeared
and filled the silent cabin

and found her, where on mornings such as this
that begged no more than attention,
she went about her chores and listened
for the imperceptible

today, it was the soft rumbling
of distant thunder – a sign
she had come to recognize
as a young girl walking alongside the sea –

a change was coming
an approaching storm:

bruised sky spread out across the water
the flapping and dropping
of the fishermen's sails
the gathering momentum of a sudden gale
and always, the summoning of dark clouds
back into the arms of that far-off tomb

even as a child
she had dreamt about that tomb

THE LENTEN MOON

where, unlike her elders,
she had always believed
the light had settled
and waited
was waiting now

to light the torches
on the changed forever shore

near Ephesus, at Mary Magdalene's table
[after Georges de la Tours *The Repentant Mary,* Oil on Canvas]

      I
in the stygian night
behind the broken crockery
of her past
she searches the less frequented alleys of her mind

for places where there might still be
traces of light

like those mornings in childhood when
the sun waited like a friend at her gate

or like those tufts of white silk that
milkweed spins and weaves
into its leaves
where the monarchs
can find them and feed
              and fly

white
like the robe He wore
crossing the ochre hills

      II
the crucifixions once fixed
in the soul
remain

shadows on distant hills
promissory notes, extinguished flame

but in the purpling sky, the rivers of time and memory
converge
      and move us

here at the table
the candle burns
it is almost morning
near Ephesus

III
in the road beyond
her small house – a single room
two, at most –
the minstrels passed
though they wouldn't
be called that in those days

and on those nights
after

He would sometimes return

these times are not recorded
anywhere
because she did not tell

the men with their all too ready
pens and prying, their incredulity
and ownership
their numbing fear

she made Him supper
and fetched His mother
and at that rustic table with its
slow burning flame

the three smiled again

and the minstrels passed…

...and Joseph

Which part of his story is yours
which do you carry with you
the shadows which are many
or the joys

I'm always drawn to his eyes

Were they hazel like *le bateau-atelier*
as it forged upstream
through the rushes
or deeper, earth toned, grounded, loam –
eyes that even when closed
rarely knew the balm of sleep

eyes that looked off into the distance
whenever a breeze passing through
would awaken the hand-wrought birds
he and the boy had carved and then strung
that now clattered and clinked
on the wind

Many may speak of him, but the Italians
Who blessedly celebrate life and its saints
With novenas of sensuous pastries, never forget

One man told me many years later
He never would have passed his Latin
And become a priest had it not been for
The reticent carpenter who kept all things
In order, and hidden

I imagine him today in his stillness, in the center
of that shop near the sea, and at night with his head
resting on its pillow of hand-written prayers and pleas

Seeing beyond his craft
            dreaming of the dancing

Helen Morrissey Rizzuto, author of *Evening Sky on a Japanese Screen, A Bird in Flight, in the dark curfew'd streets…Long Beach, Long Island in the aftermath* and co-author of *American by Choice – One Man's Journey,* is an award-winning poet and fiction writer. She has taught at Hofstra University, Queens College and for New York State Council on the Arts Poets-in-Public-Service, as a resident poet and author.

Presently, she conducts private workshops in poetry, fiction, character, and Ekphrasis and the Illustrated journal, both in New York City and on Long Island. Her students have gone on to win prestigious prizes from Random House, Little, Brown and Co. and other major publishing houses.

Visit her at www.helenmorrisseyrizzuto.com

This edition of
Helen Morrissey Rizzuto's *The Lenten Moon*
was designed by Grace Maher Graphic Design
www.gracemaher.com

The text is set in Stempel Garamond LT Standard.

Learning to Listen

imagine the voice
not out there on the hillside
where thousands are gathering
and cinematographers crank their cameras
as engineers ready to
record the sound

no, we rarely fall in love
with public spectacles

love starts with uncertainty
and dwells like a rose
in the trembling dark

in quiet so profound
that any sound
comes as intrusion

so imagine Him instead, out on the evening road
with His friends,
smiling at a story one of them is telling
or sharing one Himself

He loves stories
this man who knows sorrow
in her vast extravagance of faces
but sees endings as
beginnings

feel Him beside you this dark evening
when stars fill only half the sconces of the sky
and shadows are your only companions

when you have tired of so much
that even your name has been lost

listen

www.ingramcontent.com/pod-product-compliance
Lightning Source LLC
Chambersburg PA
CBHW020024050426
42450CB00005B/636